Become your OWN Bookkeeper

The DIY Bookkeeper's Guide to Financial Independence

Melissa W. Huggard

COPYRIGHT

All rights reserved. No part of this publication may be reproduced, distributed, or transmitted in any form or by any means, including photocopying, recording, or other electronic or mechanical methods, without the prior written permission from the publisher, except in the case of brief quotations embodied in critical reviews and certain other noncommercial uses permitted by copyright law.

Copyright © Melissa W. Huggard, (2024).

ACKNOWLEDGEMENT

I would like to express my sincere gratitude to the authors who have greatly influenced and contributed to the development of this book: Barbara Stanny, David Bach, Ramit Sethi, JL Collins, and Michelle Singletary.

Their writings have greatly influenced my understanding of personal finance and inspired me to pass on my knowledge and expertise to others. I am incredibly thankful for their contributions to the field and for the immense inspiration they have provided me in creating this book.

My sincere gratitude also goes out to my family, friends, and coworkers who have supported me during the entire journey. Your support, criticism, and constant faith in my talents have been tremendously helpful.

I'd like to thank all of the readers who have already started reading this book. It is your willingness to take charge of your finances and become your own bookkeeper that motivates me to keep imparting my expertise and assisting others in being financially independent.

Become your OWN Bookkeeper

CONTENTS

INTRODUCTION   7
   Unlocking Financial Independence Through Personal Bookkeeping   9

CHAPTER 1: INTRODUCTION TO BOOKKEEPING   16
   What is Bookkeeping?   18
   Understanding Financial Management   29
   Setting a Financial Goal   37

CHAPTER 2: THE ESSENTIALS OF PERSONAL BOOKKEEPING   49
   Introduction to Double-entry Bookkeeping   51
   Understanding the essence of Financial Tracking   64
   Reconciling Accounts   85

CHAPTER 3: TOOLS FOR EFFECTIVE BOOKKEEPING PERFORMANCE   97
   Introduction to Accounting Softwares   99
   Utilizing Spreadsheet for Business Finance   116
   Exploring mobile Apps for Expense Tracking   127

CHAPTER 4: FINANCIAL REPORT AND ANALYSIS   133
   Understanding Financial Reports   135
   Generating Financial Reports and Statements   138
   Setting up a Budget and planning for Financial Growth   145

CHAPTER 5: TAX MANAGEMENT AND COMPLIANCE   150
   Understanding Tax Management   152
   Understanding and Organizing Taxes   164

Filing Taxes as a Bookkeeper 171
CONCLUSION **180**

INTRODUCTION

Welcome to "Become Your Own Bookkeeper," a thorough manual created to provide you with the tools you need to take charge of your financial future. Learning the art of bookkeeping is your first step toward comprehending, controlling, and prospering in your personal finances in a world where financial literacy is the key to financial freedom.

In the future, picture yourself being able to easily make wise financial decisions, manage your expenses intelligently, and watch your income with assurance. "Become Your Own

Bookkeeper" is more than simply a book; it's a manual for achieving financial independence, a set of tools for creating a safe financial base, and a manual for realizing your full potential as a clever money manager.

This book will lead you through the fundamentals of accounting, help you become an expert in budgeting, and give you the confidence to handle your accounts like a pro with its practical examples, detailed instructions, and actionable insights. Every chapter is designed to provide you with the tools you need to take control of your financial situation and put yourself on the path to wealth, from creating financial objectives to assessing your financial health.

Come along with me as we explore the world of personal finance, solve the puzzle of bookkeeping, and go on a life-changing trip that will alter the way you see both your financial situation and your future.

Unlocking Financial Independence Through Personal Bookkeeping

The basis for achieving financial freedom is personal bookkeeping. Maintaining close tabs on your earnings, outgoings, and possessions provides you with priceless knowledge about your spending and financial behaviors. This information serves as the basis for wise decision-making, enabling you to reach your financial objectives more quickly and successfully.

Creating a system to keep track of all your financial activities is the first step towards starting your own bookkeeping. This could entail utilizing an accounting program, a spreadsheet, or even just a plain notebook and pen. The secret is to precisely document every source of income, expenditure, and asset.

- Income: Keep track of all of your profits, including dividends, interest, pay scales, bonuses, and any other type of compensation.
- Expenses: Regardless of size, classify and document each and every expense. This covers both discretionary and necessary costs, such as entertainment, eating out, and travel, as well as necessities like housing, food, and utilities.
- Assets: Enumerate everything you own, including cash on hand, investments, savings accounts, real estate, and any other priceless items.

After you have a thorough record of all of your transactions, you can start data analysis and get a clear picture of your financial situation. This includes:

• Finding Trends and Patterns in Your Income and Expense Data: Examine your income and expense information to find trends and patterns. This will assist you in understanding where your money is going and how your revenue varies.

• Determining Your Net Worth: To determine your net worth, deduct all of your liabilities, or debts, from all of your assets. This gives you a quick overview of your total financial situation.

• Assessing Your Ratios in Finance: Utilize financial ratios to evaluate your financial stability and advancement toward your objectives, such as the debt-to-income ratio and savings rate.

You can make a budget that supports your financial objectives based on the results of your financial analysis. A budget is a plan that shows you how to divide your income into different areas, like:

- Essential Costs: Accommodation, food, utilities, medical care, and transportation
- Discretionary Costs: Hobbies, entertainment, eating out, and travel
- Savings: Goals for investments, retirement savings, and emergency funds

Personal bookkeeping is not a one-time event, but rather an ongoing habit. By regularly reviewing your financial records and comparing your actual performance with your budget, you can keep an eye on how well you're doing financially. Consequently, you can: • Identify What Needs Improvement: Analyze your spending habits to identify areas where you can cut unnecessary spending or optimize your savings.

- Make Timely Adjustments: To stay on track, make timely adjustments if your actual performance differs considerably from your budget.

• Acknowledge Achievements: Monitor your development and acknowledge your accomplishments as you go. This will encourage you to stick with your budgetary objectives.
You'll have more money to invest in your future as you take charge of your finances.

• Maximize Savings: Establish an emergency fund, boost contributions to your retirement account, and allocate funds towards specific financial objectives, such as a down payment on a home or your child's education.

• Conducting thorough analysis of potential investments is essential for maximizing long-term wealth. It is important to carefully research and consider various financial instruments, including stocks, bonds, mutual funds, and more.

• Consult a professional: If necessary, work with a financial counselor to create a customized investing plan that fits your financial objectives and risk tolerance.

You can acquire the confidence and control required to safeguard your financial future by adopting personal bookkeeping and carefully managing your funds.

CHAPTER 1: INTRODUCTION TO BOOKKEEPING

Become your OWN Bookkeeper

What is Bookkeeping?

All business transactions that take place throughout a business's operation are recorded and categorized through the process of bookkeeping. Accounting includes bookkeeping, which is a crucial component that monitors a company's daily financial activities.

All financial transactions are documented in books of accounts, including sales revenue, taxes paid, interest earned, salaries and other operating costs, loans, investments, and so forth. The correctness of the company's whole accounting process depends on how bookkeeping is kept up to date.

Why is bookkeeping crucial in all businesses?

Bookkeeping, like any other accounting report, requires a source of data to be summarized. Bookkeeping tracks and records all financial transactions, which serve as the foundation for accounting. As a result, bookkeeping is essential for all businesses, large and small.

The following highlights the significance of bookkeeping:

- Bookkeeping helps you keep track of receipts and payments. Sales, purchases, and records for all other company transactions.
- It is beneficial to review the income, expenditure, and other ledger records on a regular basis.
- It offers data to generate financial reports that tell us particular information about

the firm, such as how much profit the business has made or how much the business is worth at a given point in time.

Types of Bookkeeping

Business entities can select between two types of bookkeeping systems, however some employ a combination of both.

- **The single-entry accounting method** demands one entry for each financial activity or transaction. A single-entry bookkeeping system is a simple system that a business can use to record daily revenues or generate a daily or weekly cash flow report.
- **The double-entry bookkeeping system** states that every transaction must be recorded twice. The double entry system

maintains checks and balances by recording a credit entry for each debit entry.

Principles of Bookkeeping

Recording daily financial transactions and corporate information is the primary goal of bookkeeping. The accuracy and completeness of each individual financial transaction are guaranteed by bookkeeping standards. Provide the data from which the accounts will be created as well. The following serves as the basis for the creation of all bookkeeping rules:

1. **The Principle of Revenue Recognition**: The bookkeeper's ability to identify revenue in an organization's income statement is the fundamental objective of the revenue recognition concept.

Revenue is the total amount of money, receivables, or other benefits that a business receives from its regular business activities, like selling products, providing services, and allowing outside parties to use its resources in order to earn dividends, interest, and royalties. Money received on behalf of third parties, such taxes, is not included. Commission is used to determine income in an agency partnership rather than gross cash inflow, receivables, or other factors.

2. **The Full Disclosure Principle**: This principle highlights the need for financial statements to reveal information rather than keep it hidden. This principle states that in order for users to utilize the bookkeeper, it must include all relevant and reliable information that the business claims in its financial statement. Instead

of focusing just on the legal structure of the information, its content and economic realities must be considered when analyzing and portraying it.

3. **The Matching Principle**: It states that expenses spent and income recognized within a bookkeeping period must be equal. For instance, the cost of those sales should be allocated to the same period if all of the sales for that time are recorded as revenue. Prepaid expenses, unpaid expenses, accrued revenue, and unearned revenue all need to be adjusted, according to this approach. It is not necessary to identify expenses and revenues in order to use matching. Instead of recording revenue on every transaction, the bookkeeper must only charge expenses for those that have been paid in full up to that moment. Because it concentrates on the incidence (or

accrual) of revenue and expenses rather than the time and magnitude of real cash inflows and outflows, this theory is fundamentally an accrual notion.

4. **The conservative principle**: Even in cases where bookkeepers are unclear of how to report an item, the conservative approach requires that possible costs and liabilities be documented right away. It instructs the bookkeeper to go for the option that lowers net income and asset value and to anticipate losses. Future legal actions, for instance, might be recorded as losses, while prospective gains from other sources wouldn't.

5. **The materiality principle**: This enables bookkeepers to record transactions and fix errors using their best judgment. A bookkeeper often uses the materiality notion when preparing tax returns or reconciling accounts. If the

discrepancy between the numbers and the overall size of the company is negligible, they can overlook the error. The idea of materiality is not stated in terms of thresholds, percentages, or money. The choice must be made by the bookkeepers using their professional judgment.

6. **Cost principle**: An object's value changes with time. The cost principle, however, states that an item's value has no bearing on its cost as reported in financial accounts. Think about investing in a building whose value has increased recently. The asset needs to be documented as the purchase price, nevertheless. This principle's most straightforward interpretation is that worth and cost are incompatible. Value changes will be shown by depreciation entries or a gain or loss from the sale of an asset. But, if you don't sell any assets,

you can't use your financial records to determine how much your company is worth.

7. **The monetary unit assumption:** All company transactions must be documented in a single currency, under the monetary unit assumption rule. Businesses that receive foreign payments and do global commerce will need to put in more work as a result of this. This theory requires that the purchasing power of currencies remain constant, meaning that inflation over time should not be taken into account. Therefore, you cannot include inflation in your financial statements, even if your business has been operating for thirty years.

Understanding Financial Management

Financial management is the strategic planning, arranging, directing, and managing of financial activities in an organization or institute. It also entails applying management principles to an organization's financial assets, which plays a significant role in fiscal management. Here are some of the objectives involved:

- Maintaining an adequate source of cash for the organization
- Ensure that the organization's stockholders receive good returns on their investment.
- Optimal and effective use of finances.
- Creating legitimate and safe investment opportunities.

Financial management also consists of some components. This includes:

- **Financial Planning**: This is the process of calculating an organization's capital requirements and allocating it accordingly. A financial strategy has specific core objectives, which are:
    - Determine the amount of capital required.
    - Identifying the capital organization and structure
    - Establishing the organization's financial policies and procedures
- **Financial control**: This is an important activity in financial management. Its primary function is to determine if an organization is accomplishing its

objectives or not. Financial control responds to the following questions:
- Are the organization's assets being used effectively?
- Are the organization's assets secure?
- Is management acting in the best financial interests of the company and its main stakeholders?
- **Financial decision-making:** This includes investment and finance for the organization. This department decides how the organization should raise funds, whether to issue more shares, and how profits should be allocated.

A financial manager oversees any firm's financial management department. This department has many functions, such as:

1. **Calculating the capital requirements**: The financial manager must determine how much funding an organization requires. This is determined by the firm's policies governing predicted expenses and profits. The amount required must be estimated such that the organization's earning capability grows.
2. **Capital structure formation**: After estimating the amount of capital required by the firm, a capital structure must be established. This includes both short and long-term debt-equity analyses. This is determined by the quantity of capital the firm possesses and the amount that needs to be raised from outside sources.
3. **Investing capital:** Every organization or firm must invest money in order to raise further funds and provide consistent

returns. As a result, the financial manager must spend the organization's finances in stable and successful projects.

4. **Allocation of profits:** Once the firm has generated a significant amount of net profit, it is the finance manager's responsibility to allocate it efficiently. This could entail preserving a portion of the net profit for contingency, innovation, or expansion purposes, while the remainder can be utilized to pay dividends to shareholders.

5. **Effective financial management**: This department is also in charge of efficiently managing the firm's finances. Money is needed for a variety of objectives in the business, including paying salaries and bills, managing stock, meeting liabilities, and purchasing materials or equipment.

6. **Financial control:** In addition to planning, organizing, and obtaining funds, the financial manager is responsible for controlling and analyzing the firm's finances in the short and long term. This can be accomplished with financial instruments such as financial forecasting, ratio analysis, risk management, and profit and cost control.

Importance of Financial Management

This style of management is significant for a number of reasons, including:

- Helps organizations with financial planning and money acquisition.
- Assists organizations in successfully using and allocating funds received or obtained.

- helps organizations make key financial decisions.
- helps to improve the profitability of enterprises.
- Increases the total value of businesses or organizations.
- Promotes economic stability.
- Encourages employees to save money, which helps them with their own financial planning.

Setting a Financial Goal

Our lives are significantly impacted by money. It allows us to follow our goals and objectives and provides us with a sense of security and independence. But becoming wealthy isn't enough to attain financial success; you also need to manage your money wisely and have a clear goal in mind. The cornerstone of both financial success and happiness on a personal level is setting financial goals. We will explore in detail the art and science of financial goal setting in this article, as well as how it may support you in achieving financial enlightenment, vigorous health, and spiritual serenity.

The significance of setting financial goals

Financial goals serve as a road map for your financial path throughout life. They offer direction, purpose, and motivation. Without clear goals, you may find yourself roaming aimlessly over the financial landscape, resulting in financial stress and unmet ambitions. Here are some fundamental reasons why creating financial goals is important:

1. **Clarity and Focus**: Setting financial goals will help you understand what you want to achieve. When you know exactly what you're working for, it's simpler to stay focused and make financial decisions that support your goals.

2. **Motivation**: Having clear financial goals gives you an incentive to save, invest, and budget wisely. The desire to achieve these goals

can be a tremendous motivator for your financial success.

3. **Measuring success**: Goals allow you to track your financial success. Regularly tracking your financial objectives allows you to see where you've come and make necessary modifications.

4. **Financial Security**: Meeting financial goals can lead to greater financial security, less stress, and the ability to deal with unexpected bills or crises.

5. **Long-Term Vision:** Financial objectives inspire you to think forward and plan for the future, ensuring that you're ready for retirement and other big life events.

6. **Personal Growth**: Setting and attaining financial objectives can help you gain

confidence and self-esteem. It demonstrates your capacity to manage your finances effectively.

Types of Financial Goals

Financial goals vary from person to person and can encompass a wide range of objectives. These financial objectives are typical:

1. Short-term objectives: Usually, these are targets you want to hit in the upcoming year. These can be creating an emergency fund, paying off credit card debt, or accumulating money for a trip.

2. Medium-Term Objectives: The duration of these objectives ranges from one to five years. Some instances include putting money down for a down payment on a home, launching a side gig, or funding a child's schooling.

3. **Long-term objectives:** These are those that will take place over a minimum of five years. Financial milestones, including saving for retirement, buying a dream home, or being financially independent, are often included in long-term aspirations.

4. **Lifestyle objectives:** These are those that seek to raise your standard of living generally. These could include having enough money to retire early and follow your passions, traveling the world, or saving for your ideal car.

5. **Goals for Debt Reduction**: If you have debt, setting objectives for its repayment is essential. Reaching debt-free status or making mortgage or student loan payments can be part of this.

6. **Investment Objectives**: Investing is a crucial aspect of budgeting. Creating a passive income

stream, diversifying an investment portfolio, and achieving a particular rate of return are a few examples of investment objectives.

SMART Goal Setting

Using the SMART criteria can help you make your financial targets more realistic and effective.

Specific: Clearly state and clarify your objective. Say "I want to save $3,000 for a holiday trip" rather than "I want to save money."

Measurable: You ought to be able to monitor your development and recognize when you've achieved your objective. By figuring out how much money you've saved, you may monitor your progress in the example above.

Achievable: Make sure your goals are doable and realistic. If your monthly salary barely covers your essential expenses, setting a goal to save $2,000 might be too ambitious.

Relevant: Your financial objectives should align with your long-term goals and principles. Ascertain how your objectives relate to your overall financial strategy.

Time-bound: Every goal has to be finished by a certain date. By giving yourself a deadline, you may prioritize your financial efforts and create a sense of urgency.

The Process of Setting Financial Goals

Setting financial objectives entails several critical actions. Let's look at these steps in detail:

1. **Self-Reflection**: Start by asking yourself what you really want to accomplish with your finances. Take into account your values, goals, and lifestyle. Your financial goals should be consistent with your personal and family aspirations.

2. **Prioritize Your Goals:** It's critical to prioritize your financial objectives. You may have multiple goals, but not all of them can be your primary focus at the same time. Consider which goals are most essential and applicable to your present life stage.

3. **Define your goals:** Use the SMART criteria to help you define your goals. Write them down, including the amount you want to save or invest, the time frame for accomplishing the objective, and how you intend to track your progress.

4. **Divide Goals into Milestones**: Breaking down large goals into smaller, more attainable milestones might help make the path less frightening. This can also give you a sense of accomplishment along the road.

5. **Develop an Action Plan**: Identify the steps you need to take to achieve your goals. This could include raising your income, lowering your costs, or pursuing new sources of money. Your action plan is a road map to success.

6. **Monitor and adjust**: Regularly evaluate your progress and make changes as needed. Life circumstances vary, and your goals may need to be adjusted accordingly.

7. **Maintain Accountability**: Discuss your goals with a trustworthy friend or family member who

can hold you accountable. Talking about your goals with someone you trust can provide support and motivation.

8. **Celebrate Achievements**: Recognize your accomplishments along the way. Recognizing and praising your accomplishments can help you stay motivated and on track.

CHAPTER 2: THE ESSENTIALS OF PERSONAL BOOKKEEPING

Become your OWN Bookkeeper

Introduction to Double-entry Bookkeeping

Double-entry bookkeeping is an accounting approach where each transaction is documented in two accounts. One account is debited, while another is credited. The entire debits and credits must be balanced. For example, suppose a business owner spends $1,000 on a new laptop computer. He credits $1,000 to his technological expense account and debits $1,000 from his cash account. This is because his technological expense assets are now worth $1000 more, while he has $1000 less in cash.

The double-entry approach in bookkeeping consists of three basic components. They are:

- Every business transaction or accounting entry must be recorded in at least two accounts on the books.
- For each transaction, the total debits and credits must be equal.
- Total assets must always equal total liabilities + equity (net worth or capital) of a company. Both sides of the equation must be equal (balanced).

The accounting equation, one of the essential concepts of accounting, helps to clarify the preceding. Both sides of this equation must be identical. If not, there is an error in the books.

Here's the equation: **Assets = Liabilities + Equity.**

As a result, if assets increase, so must liabilities in order for both sides of the equation to balance. For example, an e-commerce company purchases $1,000 of inventory on credit. Assets (inventory account) and liabilities (accounts due) both grow by $1,000. So both sides of the accounting equation are identical. This is represented in the books by deducting inventory and crediting accounts payable.

What are the different types of accounts?

Double-entry accounting requires the use of five types of accounts at all times:

- **Asset accounts** represent the monetary value of what a business possesses, such

as the cash in its checking account, tools/equipment, and buildings.
- **Liability accounts** reflect the amount a business owes on things like lines of credit or mortgages.
- **Equity account** is the difference between assets and liabilities, often known as the book worth of the business.
- **Income accounts** capture the money that comes in, such as revenue.
- **Expense accounts** track what you've spent your money on, such as payroll and advertising.

Your chart of accounts consists of five different sorts of accounts. The chart of accounts categorizes your company's financial transactions and is used to compile financial statements.

What are debit and credit?

In bookkeeping, debits and credits are used to make sure that an organization's books balance. Debits decrease liability, revenue, or equity accounts while increasing asset or expense accounts. On the other hand, credits do the reverse. Each debit entry in a transaction record needs to have a corresponding credit entry for the same amount of money, or vice versa. The essential elements of double-entry accounting are debits and credits. They are entries that track all of the money coming into and going out of a business, as well as the money moving back and forth between its several accounts, in the general ledger.

What's the difference between a debit and a credit?

Bookkeeping transactions that counterbalance each other are called debits and credits. Every transaction in a double-entry accounting system impacts a minimum of two accounts. In your chart of accounts, you have to credit one account when you debit one.

- A ledger used for accounting records debits on the left side only.
- Debits decrease debt, equity, and revenue accounts while increasing asset and expense accounts.

- In accounting ledgers, credits are always entered on the right side.
- Credits increase an account for debt, income, or equity while lowering an account for costs or assets.

Why Double Entry is Important

Double entry is extremely useful in business since it does the following:

1. **Provides a complete financial picture:** Small firms can utilize double-entry accounting to evaluate their financial health and rate of growth. This bookkeeping method keeps a record of every financial transaction, which helps to avoid fraud and embezzlement.

In fact, a double-entry accounting system is required for any business with more than one employee, inventory, debts, or many accounts. Businesses that fulfill any of these characteristics require the comprehensive financial picture that double-entry bookkeeping provides. This is because double-entry accounting may produce a number of critical financial reports such as a balance sheet and income statement.

2. **Helps Businesses Make Better Financial Decisions:** The financial accounts generated by double-entry bookkeeping show small businesses how successful they are and how financially robust certain aspects of their business are. You can track how much money you've spent and how well your firm is going.

The double-entry accounting system can assist you in making more informed financial decisions by giving accurate and timely information about your company's financial situation. This information can be used to make sound decisions about where to deploy resources, how much debt to incur, and whether to invest in new projects.

3. **Reduces bookkeeping errors**: When you create a balance sheet using double-entry accounting, your liabilities and equity (net worth or "capital") must match assets. If they don't, you know your books are incorrect. This failsafe warns businesses if their journal entries are incorrect. This accounting system makes it easier to detect and remedy problems. The double-entry approach is also a more visible way

to manage your books, which helps businesses stay accountable.

4. Favored by investors, banks, and buyers: Because the double-entry approach is more comprehensive and open, anyone thinking about giving your company money will be far more likely to do so if you utilize it. Double-entry bookkeeping generates reports that allow investors, banks, and possible buyers to see an accurate and complete view of your company's financial situation.

Practical instance of double entry bookkeeping

We'll use a simple example of three transactions for a fictitious company named XYD to show

how double entry accounting works. Thus, in order to guarantee accurate financial records, XYD employs double-entry bookkeeping and provides consulting services to clients.

Transaction 1: In exchange for the services, XYD gets $5,000 in cash from a client.

Debit Cash Account: Increase by $5,000.

Credit Service Revenue Account: Increase $5,000.

Transaction 2: XYD spends $500 on credit to purchase office supplies.

Debit Office Supply Account: Increase by $500.

Credit Accounts Payable: Increase by $500.

Transaction 3: To clear an outstanding invoice, XYD received $2,500 from a client.

Debit Cash Account: Increase by $2,500.

Credit Accounts Receivable account: Decrease by $2,500.

Through the use of double-entry accounting, XYD is able to guarantee the completeness and accuracy of its financial records, providing a transparent view of its performance and financial situation.

Understanding the essence of Financial Tracking

Tracking your company's finances allows you to reduce costs, plan for taxes, and uncover development prospects. Having a clear understanding of how money flows in and out guarantees that you do not suffer a shortage later on. A sudden cash shortage can hinder you from launching a new venture, hiring more people, or expanding your business in other ways. Worst of all, a lack of budgeting may lead to the extinction of your firm if you are unable to pay its basic necessities.

We'll go over the necessity of financial tracking, the different ways to track your funds, and the best tools for doing so.

What is financial tracking?

Financial tracking, also referred to as expense tracking, is the practice of monitoring your earnings and outlays, ideally on a daily basis. It is done by inputting invoices, business expenses, and receipts into an accounting ledger. Keeping track of your money is crucial to creating a business budget.

Financial tracking will eventually provide you a comprehensive picture of how money comes into and goes out of your company, enabling you to forecast your finances, reduce operating costs, and identify opportunities for growth. It can also assist you in reducing employee fraud, applying for business finance, and avoiding last-minute tax preparation. You will have no idea whether you are making a profit or a loss, without financial tracking.

Importance of tracking business expenses and income

- Regularly tracking your spending and income provides you with the most current financial information about your firm.
- Tracking your costs allows you to see how much you spend and what things you buy over time. If you ever need to reduce your spending, your receipts and accounting records might serve as a guidance.
- Keep a precise record of your income to help determine the profitability of your firm, if you can afford to expand, and where you need to improve.

Tips for tracking business spending and income

These are the actions you may take to efficiently get your business on track.

1. Open a company bank account: After you've started your firm, you'll need a safe means to segregate your business and personal finances. The first step in tracking your business spending and income is to register a business bank account.

Separate bank accounts help keep tax records structured and unique. Not all business arrangements are needed to maintain separate bank accounts. Separating funds, on the other hand, may aid in the effective tracking of income and expenses as well as tax planning.

Consider getting a company credit card to prevent combining personal and business costs and to develop business credit.

2. Choose an accounting technique: Before you can begin tracking your revenue and expenses, you must select an accounting technique.

The two primary accounting procedures are:

- Cash basis.
- Accrual Basis

The cash-basis approach is the most straightforward accounting method for small business owners. The cash approach involves recording income when it is received and expenses when a payment is made.

The accrual basis is more complicated than the cash-based method and employs extra accounting concepts. In accrual accounting, income and costs are recorded as they occur, regardless of when they are received or paid.

Consider the size of your firm while selecting your accounting approach.

3. Use an accounting system: Accounting can be a challenge for small business owners. You must accurately record your business expenses and income so that your data provides a fair picture of your company's financial situation.

Some options for tracking your income and expenses include:

- Using a spreadsheet
- Using Accounting Software

Using a spreadsheet gives you complete control over your income and expenses. However, spreadsheets can produce errors. You may be more prone to making mistakes or failing to frequently update the spreadsheet.

Consider using online accounting software to help you save time and track your income and expenses. Cloud-based software enables you or your workers to manage accounts receivable, payable, and other transactions at any time.

4. Keep track of your expenses: After you've decided how you'll record your income and expenses, you should maintain track of them on a regular basis. Tracking your spending enables you to track the progress of your company, create financial statements, keep track of deductibles, and submit tax returns.

Receipts (for example, transportation expenses) and other key records should be organized from the beginning of your small business.

Keep all receipts for any business-related purchases you or your staff make. Simplify the procedure by using the same business credit card or bank account for all purchases.

Understand which expenses are tax deductible. Phone, transportation, and entertainment expenses are some of the most prevalent tax deductions. Consult an accountant or specialist to find out whether your expenses are tax deductible.

5. Track expenses and income: To understand where your business stands, you must record business spending on a timely basis. Record your business expenses and total revenue on a regular basis, such as once a month.

Use a recordkeeping system to stay organized, manage spending and receipts quickly, and keep your firm from falling behind.

Organizing Financial Records

Despite the fact that organizing financial data isn't the most fun task, the benefits are significant. With well-organized records, you can find papers quickly, handle tax disputes with confidence, verify ownership of specific assets, maybe save money on taxes (for example, through capital gains tax evaluations), and, if necessary, enlist the help of others to manage your financial affairs.

What are Financial Records?

Documents that attest to or record business transactions are called financial records. A department of accounting needs well-organized financial records in order to function correctly. Invoices and receipts can be included in financial records at the most detailed level. The main ledger, subsidiary ledgers, and trial balance are the three categories into which financial records are separated. The balance sheet, income statement, and cash flow statements are a few of the more comprehensive examples.

Why Is Maintaining Financial Documentation Important?

There are several reasons why keeping financial records is crucial.

1. Observe the actions of your organization: Physical proof that your company is expanding at a healthy rate can be seen in financial statements, purchase reports, and audit books. It offers an authentic validation window that lets you spot flaws and create business procedures that are focused on the market. It raises the likelihood of business success, to put it another way.

2. Provide Truthful Financial Reports: All corporate documents, including profit and loss statements, balance sheets, and other financial data, can be easily accessed in their entirety using a reliable record management system. These documents are necessary to create accurate financial statements, which display the organization's total costs and profit for the specified time period (statements of income and expenses, for example). Even though the most reliable proof of your true legal assets, liabilities, and equity over a given time period can be found in complex accounting records like balance sheets.

3. Identification for Your Income Sources: Many diverse revenue streams are employed to provide financial and material benefits for various types of commercial and non-profit organizations. Income sources can help you differentiate between business and non-business receipts, as well as taxable and non-taxable income. Using modern document archiving technologies, you can locate and validate these sources of revenue with pinpoint accuracy.

4. Keep track of the deductible expenses: Systematically organizing financial paperwork will help you track every expense you've incurred for your business. If you do not keep accurate records of your costs, you risk losing or misplacing them. Furthermore, it can cause problems while filing out annual tax forms.

What Are the Different Record Organization Methods?

The following are some different methods for arranging financial documents:

1. Arrange Documents in Hard Copy Finance:

Follow these procedures to organize your financial records in hard copy:

Step 1: Get all of your financial documents together, including past-due invoices for your business license. You have to take the paperwork if it is important. First, you're going to pile things high.

Step 2: After gathering all of your financial documents, you must arrange them. Arrange the documents to be filed, thrown away, then filed again. This is a good use for trays or cartons.

Step 3: After sorting, treat each record separately and preserve its integrity.

Step 4: As new financial records come in, organize them into the appropriate boxes and treat them with care. It may be advantageous to manage your financial records on a designated day.

Step 5: Regularly clearing away your records is equally as crucial as tracking down new bills and paperwork as they come in. Examine your files and make any necessary changes.

2. Arranging Digital Finance Records: Hard copy records might occupy a lot of room. Thus, a large number of people are switching to digital. Furthermore, traditional statements are being replaced with digital ones by banks and credit card companies. You can take the following steps to keep these financial records in one place:

Step 1: On your computer or drive, create a folder and give it a suitable title.

Step 2: Scan all hard copies of financial documents, then organize them into the relevant folders.

Step 3: You can usually shred any papers or bills now that everything is digital. Government, tax, loan, and other documentation shouldn't be kept in hard copy. Similar to paper documents, you should store these in a special folder in a safe place.

The fourth step is to backup your financial data to a safe place, like an iCloud, OneDrive, flash drive, external hard drive, or OneDrive. Your documents will be safe thanks to this, even if your system breaks down.

3. Arrange Financial Documents with an App: If creating folders and categorizing your digital financial data seems too much work, personal finance applications can be of assistance. They're simple to use and fundamental. To assist you in creating a healthier budget, they also keep track of your weekly, monthly, and yearly spending. These apps' sole drawback is that you have to pay for the features and services they offer.

You'll need to put in a lot of work when you decide to manage your financial records. This takes time to manifest. Organizing your financial documents will come naturally to you once you've figured out how to accomplish it.

Reconciling Accounts

An accounting process called account reconciliation makes assurance that transactions in a business's financial records match reports from unbiased third parties. Reconciliation ensures that the two accounts are balanced at the conclusion of the reporting period and that the recorded amount leaving an account corresponds with the amount spent. Reconciliation is a tool used by accountants to clarify discrepancies between two financial documents, like a cash book and a bank statement. Any inexplicable difference between the two documents could be a sign of theft or embezzlement of funds.

Since the balances of the equity, liability, and asset accounts are carried forward annually, account reconciliation is necessary. You should compare the transactions entered into an internal record-keeping account with an external monthly statement obtained from credit card companies or banks during the reconciliation process. The account reconciliation statement should explain any discrepancies in the balances between the two records, which must match.

Two ways to Reconcile an Account

There are two main methods for reconciling an account, which are as follows:

1. Analysis of the paperwork: Examining the documentation is the most common method for account reconciliation. It requires obtaining the account data from the statements and evaluating each transaction's appropriateness. The documentation technique checks to see if the amount the company actually spends matches the amount that is reported in the account.

To make sure the money is spent appropriately, for instance, a company maintains track of all purchase receipts. The accountant found that the company had been charged ten times for a transaction that was not entered into the cash book during a reconciliation at the end of the month. For further details regarding the strange transaction, the accountant got in touch with the bank.

After realizing that the strange transaction was the result of a bank error, the bank reimbursed the company for the incorrect deductions. The amounts on the bank statement and cash book are in balance once the bank's errors are fixed.

2. Analytical review: This method of account reconciliation uses estimates of historical account activity levels to reconcile accounts. It comprises projecting the actual amount that ought to be in the account using past activity levels or other factors. The process is used to ascertain if the disparity is the result of theft or a balance sheet error.

An organization may, for instance, forecast how many bad debts will be in the accounts receivable and compare that number to the remaining amount in the allowance for dubious accounts. The past activity levels of the bad debts allowance are used to estimate the expected bad debts.

How Account Reconciliation Works

To log transactions and reconcile any differences between their cash books and bank accounts, the majority of firms employ accounting software. For transactions that were misentered, missed, or brought on by bank problems, reconciliation can, nevertheless, call for human intervention.

Performing an account reconciliation can be done in the following steps:

1. Check the differences between the bank statement and the cash book statement. Any cash book transactions that match comparable transactions on the bank statement should be marked. List all of the bank statement transactions for which there isn't any supporting documentation, like a payment receipt.

2. Record any payment made in the cash book that is not shown on the statement of the bank account. The options include using an ATM and making checks. From the bank's statement balance, the transactions must be deducted. Documenting transactions that are not included in the cash book but show up on the bank statement is a good idea. These transactions

include uncleared checks, overdrafts, ATM service fees, and check printing fees.

3. Examine the cash book and the bank statement to identify any transactions that appear in both. Check the cash book for any direct deposits and account credits that aren't showing up on the bank statement; add those amounts to the bank statement balance. The cash book balance should also be increased if deposits are shown on the bank statement but not in the cash book.

4. Verify any mistakes on the bank statement. When a check or deposit is deposited into the wrong account, there is an erroneous debit or credit on the bank statement from the bank. Even though bank mistakes are rare, the business should report any inconsistencies to the bank

right once. The adjustment is required in the bank reconciliation for the current period in order to reconcile the disparity, but the remedy will show up in the subsequent bank statement.

5. Verify the balances' equality. Once all inconsistencies between the cash book and the bank statement have been found, the amounts should match in both documents. The disparity between the company's internal records and its bank account should be explained in a bank reconciliation statement that you should prepare.

Bank Reconciliation Statement

A balance sheet's cash balance and a bank statement's equal amount are compared in a bank reconciliation statement. Whether accounting adjustments are necessary can be determined by reconciling the two accounts. The accuracy of the company's cash records is checked by routine bank reconciliations. They can also be used to identify monetary manipulation and fraud.

Process of Bank Reconciliation

To find any uncleared checks or deposits in transit, compare the company's list of issued checks and deposits with the checks mentioned on the bank statement.

- Reply any pending deposits to the cash amount shown on the bank statement.
- Take away any past-due checks. The updated bank cash balance will appear here.
- Next, add the amount of notes receivable and any interest collected to the company's ultimate cash balance.

- Any fines, NSF checks, or bank service costs should be subtracted. A revised corporate cash balance will be the outcome of this.
- The final adjusted cash balance of the business should match the adjusted bank balance after reconciliation.

CHAPTER 3: TOOLS FOR EFFECTIVE BOOKKEEPING PERFORMANCE

Become your OWN Bookkeeper

Introduction to Accounting Softwares

It can be difficult to manage your business's finances, so accounting software is necessary to keep track of how much money comes in and goes out. You spend less time entering data into the system because of the many time-saving features that quality systems offer. Depending on the platform, accounting software can significantly speed up and simplify tasks like tracking down past-due receivables, recording payments, and sending client invoices.

But depending on the provider, the program's level of sophistication varies. Some systems merely let you log in and out, but others include more sophisticated features that let you automate tasks that would otherwise need to be done by hand, like regular invoicing, daily data transfers via bank feed, and reconciliation.

What is accounting software?

There is a tool known as accounting software that enables you to monitor the movement of money throughout your organization and evaluate its overall financial health. You are able to establish purchase orders, maintain stock levels, charge customers, and view account balances. Additionally, it enables you to record transactions, generate reports, manage connections with customers and vendors, and create purchase orders. According to the words of Ken Stalcup, "using an accounting package will help organize your records and 'force' you into a systematic structure that will put the company's finances into a system that can report the financial results and help when it comes to tax time."

Why use accounting software?

Accounting software can minimize errors and save your company time. "The biggest advantage of adopting current accounting software is efficiency; you have all of your transaction information in one location instead of copying and pasting data from spreadsheet to spreadsheet," Fabien Dawidowicz said. You always know where to find it and can easily see how much has been brought into or spent by the company."

You can connect the software to your corporate bank and credit card accounts via the bank feed option, saving yourself the trouble of manually entering data and transactions. You will receive a daily update on your transactions once this is implemented. The dashboard of the majority of accounting apps shows current data on your most important metrics.

The program can be used to generate a range of reports and financial statements, such as profit and loss statements and balance sheets, which are required when asking investors for money. To make informed business decisions and plan for the future, you can also compare transaction history or statement comparisons between your current and past months and years to assess your company's growth, sales patterns, and other vital data.

Accounting software can assist you with scheduling payments and organizing your expenses, regardless of whether you pay your bills online, with a credit card, check, or cash.

As a result, you'll be able to keep an eye on the transactions and manage your cash flow.

The software also allows you to record cash or check payments, as well as produce and send invoices and past-due warnings.

Accounting software automates many tiresome and repetitive accounting activities, increasing data accuracy and making bookkeeping more efficient. If you utilize cloud accounting software, you can do your accounting from anyplace with a signal.

Key advantages of using accounting software:

1. Billing and invoicing: These two crucial business operations account for the majority of your company's income. Manually processing invoices is time-consuming, labor-intensive, and error-prone. When you have recurring orders, it is not feasible to produce paper invoices for each transaction your client completes with you. Without automated systems, it is difficult to stay on top of bills and remind clients when payments are past due.

Accounting software offers solutions that efficiently handle these problems and streamline the invoicing process. For clients that place orders frequently, you can create recurring profiles and schedule invoices to be sent out automatically each time an order is placed. You can include terms and conditions on your invoices to inform your clients about payments. Accounting software allows for the automation of payment reminders. You can plan reminders to be sent to your clients automatically via the program, based on projected dates for invoice due dates or payments. Using an accounting tool will help you keep track of all your outstanding bills, remind customers to pay on time, and avoid unintentional payment problems.

2. Online payments: After you've billed your clients, the following step is to get paid. It could be daunting if clients aren't provided with a reliable method of collecting payments.

Integrating your accounting system with a variety of online payment gateways enables you to provide clients with a quick and safe method of making payments. Payment gateways automatically update your accounting system and log payments under the appropriate invoice. They also provide a variety of payment options to their clients, including credit and debit cards as well as online bank transfers.

With a global customer, your company must be capable of handling many currencies. With online payment gateways that are integrated with your accounting software and support many currencies, you can take payments in the currencies of your clients while still handling your own accounts. Errors and additional calculations related to international transactions are eliminated by doing this.

3. Expense tracking: Keeping track of your costs is essential to comprehending your financial flow. Accounting software helps you keep tabs on and organize your expenses so you can see exactly where your money is going. Accounting software can also be used to automatically scan, upload, and enter data from expense receipts. As a result, there is no longer any need to save paper receipts and no chance of losing them. Billing consumers for charges incurred on their behalf is made simple by accounting software.

4. Bank reconciliation: Accounting software makes bank reconciliation easier. It's a basic accounting function of any business. You can obtain bank feed statements into your accounts right away by directly connecting your bank account to accounting software. You may automatically match and classify imported bank transactions using the custom criteria and bank rules built into your accounting software. Reconcile your accounts by only verifying and confirming the transactions once they match. Bank reconciliation is made simpler by accounting software, which also keeps your company audit-ready all year long.

5. Project management and timesheets: An effective accounting program should have a timesheets module that lets you bill clients according to the amount of time you spend on a project. Timesheets facilitate project management by assisting with planning, recording time, and invoicing clients. You may avoid charging your clients too much or too little by using accounting software to measure the amount of time spent on tasks. To make sure everyone is in agreement, you might even ask your clients to validate your time entries before charging them. Timesheets let you compare your actual hours worked to your initial budget when a project is finished, which helps you make better plans for the future.

6. Inventory Management: An essential part of any company is inventory management. Sufficient inventory control is necessary to keep a sufficient supply on hand and deliver excellent customer support. It comprises accounting, tracking items, recording item information, and producing reports. Accounting software is helpful for creating bundles, adding photographs to items, tracking the flow of goods by batch or serial number, and entering Stock Keeping Unit (SKU) codes. When you get an order for goods, you can create a sales order using your accounting software, turn it into an invoice once it has been approved, and then apply the relevant taxes. To make sure you never run out of stock, you may establish reorder thresholds, monitor stock levels, and receive automated emails for your products. In order to gain a deeper comprehension and improve inventory management, you can also generate reports that are particular to inventory.

7. Compliance: An excellent accounting program should make it simple to file taxes and follow state and municipal tax laws. You may compute taxes more quickly and easily when using accounting software when dealing with different tax rates. It can also help you stay organized and prepared for tax season by providing tax summary reports, which will aid in your knowledge of your taxes.

8. Creation of reports: You, the owner, need to frequently evaluate your company's growth and make informed decisions if you want to secure its long-term success. Accounting reports give you insight into your company's development and financial patterns. Making reports with spreadsheets is time-consuming nevertheless, as each report needs to have manual data consolidation and formula entry. Accounting software automatically generates reports, which saves you time and effort. The balance sheet, the profit and loss statement, and the cash flow statement are the three key financial statements that each and every business must understand. Reporting features in accounting software help businesses monitor and control their cash flow. You can grasp your company's key financial features, draw inferences, and make actions that will move it in the right direction by creating profit and loss statements and balance sheet reports. An accounting system automatically compiles information on various crucial aspects of your business, like sales, purchases, taxes, inventories, and projects, in addition to the three primary financial statements. With the aid of all this data, you can maintain the health of your firm, generate reports instantly, and make decisions quickly.

Examples of Accounting Software

These are some examples of the accounting softwares currently available that you may use to help your company's bookkeeping:

- Patriot Software
- Oracle NetSuite
- Quickbooks
- FreshBooks
- Zoho Books
- 1-800Accountant
- Quicken
- Neat
- Decimal

Utilizing Spreadsheet for Business Finance

Because the world of business is fraught with continual financial commitments and unforeseen expenses, successfully managing personal finances has become essential. While the classic pen-and-paper method may still be useful for some, technology has provided us with a valuable tool that is frequently overlooked: spreadsheets. Spreadsheets are effective tools for streamlining financial processes, such as budgeting and forecasting.

What is a spreadsheet?
A spreadsheet is a software application that facilitates tabular data organization, analysis, and manipulation. In a spreadsheet, each cell can

contain text, numbers, or mathematical algorithms. Spreadsheets are a common tool for financial reporting, data analysis, forecasting, and budgeting. It can also be compared to computer software that facilitates the entry, modification, and analysis of data in tabular form by users. It is made up of a grid of rows and columns, with data—such as text, numbers, or formulas—in each intersection, or cell. Spreadsheets are frequently used for data management, financial analysis, and budgeting. A word processor is more of a tool for presenting what you know, whereas a spreadsheet makes it simple to perform what-if calculations, according to Dan Bricklin, one of the developers of VisiCalc, one of the earliest spreadsheet systems.

Importance of Spreadsheet in Business

1. Planning and Budgeting: Exact budgets for various projects or departments can be created using spreadsheets. Businesses may keep an eye on their financial situation and make informed decisions by tracking their income and expenses. Spreadsheets make budgeting more accurate and efficient by using formulas and functions to automatically calculate totals, percentages, and variances.

2. Financial Analysis: Trends, patterns, and anomalies can be found in financial data by using spreadsheets to analyze it. Companies can use this information to improve their financial performance and make strategic decisions.Financial data can be visually represented by spreadsheets through the creation of charts and graphs, which facilitates understanding and interpretation.

3. Forecasting and Projection: By utilizing historical data, spreadsheets may be utilized to forecast future financial performance. This makes it possible for enterprises to anticipate challenges and opportunities. Companies can model a variety of situations to assess how different events might affect their cash flow and plan for emergencies.

4. Financial Reporting: Cash flow, revenue, and balance sheets are just a few of the financial reports that may be generated using spreadsheets. These reports offer a thorough summary of the financial status of the business. Reports can be customized by businesses to meet their needs, with data added or removed as necessary.

5. Data Management: Excel spreadsheets are an excellent tool for organizing and storing large amounts of financial data. Companies can easily access and update data, which lowers the chance of mistakes. Businesses can examine data from multiple perspectives and gain valuable insights into their finances by using filters and sorting capabilities.

6. Cooperation and Sharing: To promote cooperation on financial tasks, team members can share spreadsheets. The ability for multiple users to collaborate on the same spreadsheet at once boosts productivity. Spreadsheets hosted on the cloud allow businesses to access data from any location, guaranteeing that all users have access to the most recent information.

7. Risk Management: Spreadsheets are a useful tool for recognizing and controlling financial hazards. Businesses can identify potential hazards and create risk management plans with the help of data analysis. Spreadsheets can be used by firms to assess key risk indicators and regularly monitor their financial health.

Using Excel spreadsheet for company finance

We've already seen how important spreadsheets are in business. There are various spreadsheet applications that can help you with your business venture, but we will focus on Excel. Excel's versatility and functionality make it an excellent tool for commercial finance.

Let me demonstrate how Excel may be utilized for business finance using this scenario:

Assume you own a small consulting business and want to build a budget for the future year. You've evaluated your income and costs and want to utilize Excel to organize the data and calculate your expected profit. Here are the steps to follow:

Step 1: Set Up the Spreadsheet

Open Excel and make a new spreadsheet.

In cell A1, make "Item" the header for your first column.

In cell B1, type "Estimated Cost" as the header for your second column.

In cell C1, type "Actual Cost" as the header for your third column.

In cell D1, enter "Difference" as the fourth column header.

Step 2: Enter Income and Expenses

Starting with cell A2, enter the things for which you intend to produce money or incur expenses in column A (for example, "Consulting Fees," "Office Rent," "Utilities," "Marketing").

In column B, beginning with cell B2, enter the estimated cost for each item. Enter positive values for income and negative values for costs.

Once expenses begin to accumulate, you can enter actual charges in column C.

Step 3: Calculate the Total

To determine the total expected income and expenses, enter the formula "=SUM(B2:B12)" into cell B13 (or any empty cell below your data).

In cell C13, enter the formula "=SUM(C2:C12)" to compute the total actual revenue and expenses.

Step 4: Calculate the Difference

In cell D2, insert the formula "=C2-B2" to compute the difference between the first item's estimated and actual costs.

Copy this formula down to the remaining items in column D.

Step 5: Analyze the Budget

Use conditional formatting to emphasize positive differences (increased revenue) in green and negative differences (increased expenses) in red. Make a simple chart to visualize your budget, comparing estimated and real expenditures for each transaction.

Step 6: Review and Adjust

To track your financial performance, keep your budget updated on a regular basis with actual revenue and expenses. Using Excel's tools, you may examine variations, discover trends, and make informed budget adjustments as needed.

By using Excel in this manner, you can develop a detailed budget for your business, track your financial performance, and make informed decisions to improve your company's financial health.

Exploring mobile Apps for Expense Tracking

Exploring mobile apps for expense tracking can revolutionize the way you manage your finances. These apps offer a myriad of features designed to simplify the process of tracking, categorizing, and analyzing expenses.

Let's delve deeper into some popular options:

1. **Expensify**: Renowned for its intuitive interface and advanced functionality, Expensify is a versatile tool suitable for personal and business use. It excels in automating expense tracking through receipt scanning, automatic

categorization, and seamless integration with accounting software. Additionally, Expensify offers features like mileage tracking and real-time expense reporting, making it a comprehensive solution for managing expenses on the go.

2. **QuickBooks Online**: While primarily an accounting software, QuickBooks Online offers a mobile app that extends its capabilities to expense tracking. The app seamlessly syncs with your bank accounts and credit cards, allowing you to effortlessly track and categorize expenses in real time. Moreover, QuickBooks Online provides insightful reports and analytics, empowering you to make informed financial decisions.

3. **Zoho Expense**: As part of the Zoho suite of business tools, Zoho Expense offers a robust set of features tailored for efficient expense

management. From receipt scanning to mileage tracking, Zoho Expense simplifies the process of tracking and reimbursing expenses for employees. Its integration with other Zoho applications enhances its utility, making it a valuable asset for businesses seeking a comprehensive expense management solution.

4. Receipts by Wave: Wave's Receipts app is designed to streamline receipt and expense management for small businesses and freelancers. The app allows you to digitize receipts, track mileage, and generate expense reports effortlessly. Its integration with Wave's accounting features ensures seamless synchronization of expense data, enabling you to maintain accurate financial records.

5. Shoeboxed: Specializing in receipt and expense tracking, Shoeboxed offers a convenient way to organize and manage your expenses. The app's receipt scanning feature digitizes receipts, eliminating the need for manual entry. Additionally, Shoeboxed provides tools for tracking mileage and generating expense reports, making it a comprehensive solution for individuals and businesses alike.

6. Mint: Mint's comprehensive personal finance app includes robust expense tracking features. Beyond basic expense categorization, Mint provides insights into your spending habits and offers personalized recommendations for optimizing your finances. Its bill tracking feature ensures you never miss a payment, further enhancing its utility as a holistic financial management tool.

Become your OWN Bookkeeper

CHAPTER 4: FINANCIAL REPORT AND ANALYSIS

Understanding Financial Reports

Financial reports are important documents that provide an overview of a company's financial health and performance. They help stakeholders—including creditors, investors, and management—assess the company's financial health and make wise decisions. This holds particular significance for small enterprises, as it provides insightful data regarding their operational and fiscal well-being.

Types of Financial Report

1. Equilibrium Reports: A company's financial situation as of a particular date is displayed on its balance sheet. Liabilities, assets, and shareholder equity make up its composition. Money, products, and real estate make up the corporation's assets. Liabilities include things like outstanding loans and accounts payable for the business. Equity held by shareholders represents the owners' legitimate claim to the company's assets. Liabilities + Shareholder Equity = Assets is the formula for the balance sheet.

2. Income statement: This is also called the profit and loss statement, it provides a snapshot of a company's financial performance over a certain period of time. Net income, costs, and revenue make up its components. Revenues are the earnings generated by a business's main activities, such as sales. Expenses are the costs incurred in generating revenue, such as salary and rent. The income statement's formula is Net Income = Revenues - Expenses.

3. Cash Flow Statements: The cash flow statement illustrates how adjustments to income and balance sheet accounts affect cash and its equivalents. The three divisions are for operating, investing, and financing activities. Operating activities are the company's cash flows from its main business operations. Cash flows from asset sales and purchases are a part of investment operations. Financing operations include the financial flows from repayment and capital raising.

4. Financial ratios: These are metrics used to assess an organization's performance and financial health. Pattern detection, performance comparison with industry peers, and assessing a company's capacity to pay its debts are among the tasks they can assist with. Common financial measures include yield ratios (like net margin, gross margin), liquidity ratios (like quick and current ratios), and leverage ratios (like interest coverage and debt-to-equity ratios).

Generating Financial Reports and Statements

For organizations to assess their financial health and make wise decisions, accurate and timely financial reporting is essential. These are the steps involved in producing a financial report.

1. Compile financial information: Gather any relevant financial information, including bank statements, asset and liability data, and records of income and expenses.

2. Get statements of finances ready: Spreadsheet tools or accounting software should be used to prepare cash flow, income, and balance sheets.

3. Examine and evaluate: Verify the accuracy of the financial statements and conduct an analysis to get understanding of the company's financial situation.

4. Produce corroborating documentation: To provide context and explanation, prepare supporting documents such as the management discussion and analysis (MD&A) and notes to the financial statements.

5. Distribute financial reports: To keep stakeholders informed about the company's financial status, distribute financial reports to lenders, investors, and management.

Financial Analysis Techniques for Business

Financial analysis allows business owners to better understand their financial performance and find opportunities for improvement. You can utilize the following techniques:

1. Ratio Analysis: Financial ratios are calculated and interpreted to measure many aspects of a company's financial performance. Common business ratios include the current ratio (current assets/current liabilities), the quick ratio (quick assets/current liabilities), and the debt-to-equity ratio.

2. Trend analysis: This entails analyzing financial data across time to detect patterns and trends. Business owners can use trend analysis to monitor the growth of key financial measures and discover areas for improvement.

3. Budget variance analysis: It identifies disparities between actual financial outcomes and budgeted amounts. Business leaders can utilize this study to figure out why actual outcomes differ from predictions and then alter their budgets accordingly.

4. Benchmarking: This means comparing a company's financial performance and ratios to those of its industry peers or competitors. It can assist in identifying areas where the organization is excelling or falling behind. For example, comparing a company's return on equity (ROE) to the industry average might reveal how efficiently it uses shareholder cash.

5. Horizontal and Vertical Analysis: Horizontal analysis examines financial data over different time periods (such as quarters or years) to determine growth or decline. Vertical analysis compares each line item in the financial statements to a base item to determine their relative proportion. For example, comparing the current year's revenue to the prior year's revenue reveals the growth rate.

Using Financial Reports For Decision Making

Financial reports help firms make educated decisions about their operations, investments, and growth strategies.

1. Investment Decisions: Financial reports help organizations analyze investment options and assess prospective returns.

2. Cost Control initiatives: Financial reports can help discover areas of cost inefficiency and design cost-cutting initiatives.

3. Risk management: It involves identifying and mitigating financial risks such as liquidity, solvency, and profitability.

Setting up a Budget and planning for Financial Growth

Budgeting is an important part of business financial planning since it allows them to allocate resources more effectively and achieve their financial goals. Before creating a budget, firms should specify their financial objectives, such as growing revenue, lowering spending, or improving profitability. These goals will drive the budgeting process and keep businesses on track.

Steps to Creating a Budget for Financial Growth

Setting up a budget requires numerous stages to ensure that it is practical and in line with the company's financial objectives.

1. Gather financial data: Collect historical financial data, such as income statements, balance sheets, and cash flow statements, to better evaluate prior performance and patterns.

2. Determine revenue sources: Determine all sources of money, such as sales, investments, and other sources of income, in order to project future revenue.

3. Estimate expenses: Add up all fixed (rent, salaries, etc.) and variable (raw materials, utilities, etc.) prices to determine overall expenses.

4. Make a spreadsheet for your budget: Using a spreadsheet program, create a template for your budget that has columns for income, expenses, and net income for every month or quarter.

5. Allocate resources: Allocate resources depending on the company's financial objectives, ensuring that adequate money is provided to important areas that promote growth.

6. Monitor and adjust: Monitor actual financial performance versus the budget on a regular basis and adjust as needed to keep on track to meet financial goals.

Planning for Financial Growth

Once a budget is established, firms can utilize it to prepare for future financial growth.

1. Investment Planning: Use the budget to prepare for growth-oriented initiatives such as expanding operations, launching new products, or entering new markets.

2. Cost Control Strategies: Determine where costs can be lowered or optimized in order to increase profitability and free up funds for expansion efforts.

3. Revenue Growth techniques: Create revenue-generating techniques like marketing campaigns, sales promotions, and customer acquisition.

4. Risk Management: Use the budget to identify and reduce financial risks such as cash flow shortfalls, market changes, and unanticipated costs.

CHAPTER 5: TAX MANAGEMENT AND COMPLIANCE

Become your OWN Bookkeeper

Understanding Tax Management

Tax management is the strategic planning and implementation of steps aimed at improving a company's tax situation while adhering to tax rules and regulations. It entails a variety of tasks, including tax planning, risk assessment, and tax compliance, all with the purpose of lowering tax liabilities and increasing tax advantages for the company. Tax management includes both proactive and reactive strategies to reduce tax liabilities and solve tax-related risks and issues effectively.

Importance of Tax Management

1. Minimizes Tax liabilities: Effective tax management enables individuals and organizations to lawfully reduce their tax bills by utilizing tax deductions, credits, incentives, and planning tactics. This leads to lesser tax payments, saving more income and profits.

2. Maximizes Tax Benefit: Individuals and corporations can maximize their tax benefits by arranging their finances and operations in a tax-efficient manner. This could include selecting the appropriate business structure, investment vehicles, retirement funds, and timing revenue and expenses to lower taxable income.

3. Improves Cash Flow: Efficient tax management can boost cash flow by reducing the impact of tax payments on liquidity. Businesses can guarantee they have enough cash on hand to pay their financial responsibilities while still pursuing development prospects by planning for tax requirements and optimizing timing techniques.

4. Assures Compliance: To prevent penalties, fines, and legal repercussions, one must comprehend and abide by tax laws and regulations. By staying up to date with tax regulations and completing their tax obligations precisely and on time, individuals and companies can avoid audits and investigations.

5. Supports Financial Planning: Tax management is crucial for financial planning because it makes tax obligations clear and foreseeable. Taxes are taken into account while making plans for retirement, both individuals and companies can make better decisions on investing, saving, and budgeting.

Elements of Tax Management:

- **Tax planning** is the process of organizing corporate transactions and operations in order to legally reduce tax payments.
- **Tax compliance** entails meeting tax duties, such as submitting returns and paying taxes on time

Tax Planning Strategies for Business

Tax planning is an important part of corporate financial management since it allows them to reduce their tax bills while increasing their tax benefits. Here are some tax planning measures that firms can consider:

1. Structure Optimization: Selecting the appropriate business entity structure (e.g., sole proprietorship, partnership, corporation, S corporation) might affect tax requirements. Each structure has various tax ramifications, therefore firms should choose which structure best fits their tax planning objectives.

2. Capital investment Planning: Using tax breaks for capital expenditures, such as bonus depreciation and Section 179 deductions, can assist firms reduce taxable income and lower tax liability in the year the investment is made.

3. Timing of Income and Expenses: Taxable income may be affected by the timing of income and expenses. One way to reduce taxable income and tax obligations is to defer revenue to a future tax year or accelerate deductions into the current year.

4. Inventory Management: The cost of goods sold (COGS) and inventory valuation can be impacted by the use of inventory management techniques like the last-in, first-out (LIFO) or first-in, first-out (FIFO) method, which in turn can affect taxable income.

5. **Employee Benefit Planning**: Employers can reduce their tax burden and attract and retain talent by providing tax-advantaged benefits like flexible spending accounts (FSAs), health savings accounts (HSAs), retirement plans (like 401(k) and SEP IRAs), and fringe benefits (like educational assistance and transportation benefits).

Tax Compliance for Businesses

Tax compliance for businesses entails following all applicable tax rules, regulations, and requirements established by federal, state, and municipal tax authorities. Here are some important components of tax compliance for businesses:

1. Filing Tax Returns: Businesses must submit accurate and timely tax returns, such as income tax returns (Form 1120 for corporations, Form 1065 for partnerships), employment tax returns (Form 941 for quarterly payroll taxes), and sales tax returns (which vary by state).

2. Record-Keeping: Accurate and complete records of financial activities, income, spending, deductions, and supporting documentation are required for tax compliance and to substantiate tax deductions or credits claimed on tax returns.

3. Payment of Taxes: Businesses must pay all taxes owed in accordance with applicable tax laws and regulations. This includes income taxes, payroll taxes, sales taxes, and any other taxes levied against the business.

4. Estimated Taxes: Businesses may be compelled to make anticipated tax payments throughout the year if they expect to owe a specific amount of tax. This includes income taxes and self-employment taxes for certain business companies.

5. Depositing Taxes: Employers are expected to deposit payroll taxes, such as federal income tax withholding, Social Security tax, and Medicare tax, on a regular basis in accordance with the IRS' deposit schedule.

6. Compliance with Tax rules: Businesses must follow all applicable tax rules and regulations, including federal, state, and local taxes. This involves comprehending and complying with tax deadlines, filing requirements, and any special laws or restrictions that relate to their commercial activity.

7. Requirements: Businesses must accurately and thoroughly record certain taxable events, transactions, and financial information on their tax returns, as well as any other applicable forms and schedules.

Understanding and Organizing Taxes

The taxes that businesses are required to pay on their income, gains, and operations are referred to as business taxes. The federal, state, and local governments levy these taxes, which are then utilized to fund public operations and services. One of the most crucial aspects of managing a business is paying taxes.

Types of Business Taxes

1. Income taxes: Federal, state, and occasionally local governments impose taxes on business profits.

2. Employment taxes: These comprise state and federal unemployment insurance taxes, Medicare and Social Security taxes, and state disability insurance taxes.

3. Sales taxes: A tax imposed on the exchange of goods and services, these are gathered by companies and then given back to the taxing body.

4. Property taxes: Usually paid to local governments, these are imposed on business-owned real and personal property.

Organizing Income Tax for Businesses

Income taxes are one of the most important taxes for businesses, affecting both profitability and cash flow.

- **Taxable Income Calculation**: To calculate taxable income, subtract permitted deductions from gross income. Understand the various tax rates and brackets that apply to different amounts of taxable income.
- **Tax credit and deductions**: Take advantage of various tax advantages and deductions for businesses, such as R&D credits, investment tax credits, and business cost deductions.

Organizing Employment Taxes for Businesses

Employing businesses are subject to employment taxes.

- Classification of Employees: Recognize the differences between independent contractors and employees because each has specific tax obligations. Make sure payroll taxes are deducted and sent to the appropriate taxing authorities, and that employee earnings are reported truthfully.
- Requirements for filing and reporting: On schedule, fill out the necessary employment tax forms. Keep thorough records of all employment taxes that have been recorded and paid.

Organizing Sales and Property Taxes for Businesses

Two other kinds of taxes that firms must manage well are sales and property taxes.

- **Gathering and Reporting Sales Taxes**: Get sales tax from customers and send it to the relevant taxing body for any taxable sales. Make sure you timely file all required sales tax returns and reports, and that you accurately record the sales tax that is collected and returned.
- **Assessment and Remittance of Property Tax**: Find out how property taxes are assessed and paid by the business's jurisdiction. Make sure you pay your property taxes on schedule and that you

seek for and take advantage of any exemptions or abatements that may be available.

Filing Taxes as a Bookkeeper

Filing taxes is a crucial aspect of your work as a bookkeeper since it guarantees that your customer or business complies with tax laws. It is imperative that you:

- Find out which business entities—such as corporations, partnerships, and sole proprietorships—need to file taxes.
- Recognize the deadlines for submitting many tax forms and the consequences of missing them.
- Organize and keep accurate records of every client's earnings, outlays, deductions, and other pertinent financial data.

- To support taxes, keep track of documents pertaining to taxes, such as W-2s, 1099s, and receipts.

Tax Preparation and Calculation

Tax preparation and calculation are essential activities for bookkeepers when submitting taxes for their clients. As a business owner who also serves as your own bookkeeper, you must comprehend this.

1. **Gathering financial information**: Gather all pertinent financial information for each client, such as income statements, balance sheets, and expense reports. Before filing your tax returns, double-check that all of

your financial information is correct and current.

2. **Calculating taxable income**: To calculate taxable income, subtract permitted deductions from gross income. Calculate the total tax liability by applying the applicable tax rates and brackets.

Let's use a simple example to show how to prepare and compute income tax for a business:

DDG Bakery is a small business that sells bread and pastries from its bakery. At the end of the year, the bakery must determine its income tax due based on taxable income.

Step 1: Determine taxable income.

1. Calculate gross revenue: Add up the bakery's total sales revenue for the year. Assume DDG Bakery's gross revenue is $150,000.

2. Subtract the cost of goods sold (COGS): Calculate the cost of ingredients, labor, and other direct costs associated with creating the goods sold. Let's say DDG Bakery's COGS is $50,000.

3. To calculate gross profit, subtract COGS from gross revenue: $150,000 - $50,000 = $100,000.

4. Deduct Other Operating Expenses: This includes rent, utilities, salaries, and advertising charges. Assume DDG Bakery's total operating expenses are $30,000.

5. Gross Profit - Operating Expenses is operating income, which is determined as $100,000 - $30,000 = $70,000.
6. Allowable deductions include depreciation, interest expenses, and other eligible business expenses. Let's say DDG Bakery's deductions total $5,000.
7. To calculate taxable income, subtract operating income from deductions. For example, $70,000 minus $5,000 equals $65,000.

Step 2: Calculate Tax Liability.

1. Determine the Tax Rate: Consult the current tax brackets and rates for businesses. Assume DDG Bakery's

taxable income is in the 20% tax rate for small companies.

2. Calculate tax liability: Multiply the taxable income by the appropriate tax rate. DDG Bakery's tax liability is calculated as: Tax Liability = Taxable Income × Tax Rate = \$65,000 × 20% = \$13,000.

Step 3: Additional Considerations.

1. Estimated payments: To prevent fines for underpayment, estimate quarterly tax payments based on estimated annual revenue.

2. Credits and deductions: Consider any available tax credits or deductions that may further lower your tax liability, such

as R&D credits or small company deductions.

Filing Tax Returns

Bookkeepers' tax filing process concludes with the filing of tax returns. Here's how to file tax returns correctly and efficiently.

1. Fill out the appropriate tax forms, such as Form 1040 (Individual Income Tax Return) or Form 1120 (Corporate Income Tax Return), depending on the client's company type.
2. Before filing, double-check all information on the tax forms to ensure its accuracy.

3. Determine whether to e-file or paper-file tax returns depending on the client's choices and IRS standards.
4. Ensure that e-filed returns are submitted securely and contain all required information.

Ensuring Tax Compliance

We've already explored how bookkeepers must ensure tax compliance when submitting taxes for their clients. These are some steps to assure tax compliance while reducing the risk of audits and penalties.

- Review tax returns thoroughly to ensure that all information is correct and complete.

- Double-check your figures to ensure that all deductions and credits are legitimate.
- Keep copies of each client's tax returns and accompanying paperwork for a minimum of three years.
- Organize documentation so that it is easy to locate and retrieve when needed.

CONCLUSION

Being an expert in bookkeeping is more than just keeping track of figures—it means being in charge of your business's financial destiny. With its comprehensive coverage of double-entry accounting principles and intricate details of tax management and compliance, this book will arm you with the knowledge and resources necessary to adeptly maneuver through the intricate realm of business finance.

You have given yourself the power to make informed decisions, enhance financial performance, and accomplish your business goals by taking on the role of self-employed bookkeeper. The ideas in this book will act as a reliable road map for every entrepreneur, regardless of experience level, since they will help you achieve success.

Keep in mind that bookkeeping is a mindset, a discipline, and a tactical advantage rather than merely a task that needs to be finished. Accept it, refine it, and allow it to drive you toward more achievement and advancement.

May you embark on your journey with determination, clarity, and purpose as you put this book away. You control your financial future, so seize the chance to grow your business to its fullest and rise to the challenge.

Become your OWN Bookkeeper

Become your OWN Bookkeeper

www.ingramcontent.com/pod-product-compliance
Lightning Source LLC
Chambersburg PA
CBHW071502220526
45472CB00003B/887